Cruelty and Transformation:
the integration of mysticism in life and art

by Graham Cwinn

"There may, or may not, be a future for humanity as we know it, but either way the time has come for us sorcerers to transform the pessimism of our world into a profound acknowledgement of mystery."

— Gast Bouschet

"But no matter how loudly we clamor for magic in our lives, we are really afraid of pursuing an existence entirely under its influence and sign."

— Antonin Artaud

"Standing skinned and naked in life is a powerful spiritual and often necessary experience. Being left alone without support in these moments is not."

— Frater Acher

"We need to work until the end of time
 We need to rediscover the Gesture and the Word."

— Jacques Prevel

Mysticism. Spirituality. Magic.

When most people hear these words, they tune out or back away. I, for a long time, became one of the many who fled from these notions.

As time marches on, I have found within myself an emptiness, profound and resolute: a hole carved ever-wider by trauma and mental illness.

Over the past two years, while waiting for an important medical procedure, I have given much consideration to this feeling of emptiness and how I can live with it.

Also during this time, I have been re-invigorating my passion for reading: primarily I rekindled my passion for one of the greatest humans to ever live, Antonin Artaud. My obsession, my endless poring over of his works, sparked a small flame somewhere deep in the recesses of that empty hole in me. I began to realize that my illness and trauma, while a part of me, do not define me; however, they have created barriers within me, separating me from myself and the world around me.

These barriers have to be shattered: but, how? As I continued to read Artaud, other important artists and writers (both older and contemporary) came to my attention. The reasons that drew me to them were many, I will list two:

First, like Artaud, these marvelous humans speak of the cruelty, the pain, inherent to existence, and how this cruelty can shape and distort us. What's important to note is that these artists do not revel in their pain, in this cruelty: rather, it is seen as a **transformative** *element.*

Second, they all speak of the necessity to return to magic and ritual as a way of mitigating or reducing the cruelty we experience and (intentionally or unintentionally) pass on to others: this, here, was a way to brighten that flame within me, to illuminate the hole carved by cruelty, and in doing so, perhaps I will discover my true self and feel reconnected to the world.

This rekindled my desire to follow the path of mysticism and spirituality. I have concluded, during this time, that art itself is a form of magic, that my poetry is magic: I use my will to create a conduit between my soul and the souls of others, in attempt to evoke a sense of wonder and inclu-

sion in them, so as to realize we are all One.

My hope is that by using poetry as incantation, I can help eliminate even a fraction of loneliness in this world.

for those who are lost.

at the altar of Our First Lady Exhaustion

I have journeyed for thousands of kilometers —
harrowing cliffs, humid valleys, bitter winters
— to at last arrive at this holy place of worship.

yet I have not come to pray, or give thanks.

I am here to weep in dejection and despair;
to beg for relief from the egrets that flock to
the bags under my eyes, and the shadows
that stalk me perpetually;

to spit in rage at her alabaster feet
for cursing me with the endless nights
that turn to endless days in a horrible
cycle where I never find rest.

"it will make you stronger."

I didn't need to be tough.
I needed to be safe.

now there are holes in me
that might never be filled;
that I must learn to grow
around.

I must rediscover the infinite in everything.

stasis

an interstitial space
between my world and yours

we wept together beneath a sycamore

am I gestating or stagnating?

lost in moments

an embrace			the creaking walls

a shared laugh		the dripping tap

the trauma from sexual abuse

and			five suicide attempts

you, soaked in blood, screaming
that you wanted to die

our wails, melting into sirens

will this ever end?

wounds

we once were ashamed
of our own suffering,

and we would wear
cloaks, like lepers,
to hide the marks
on our bodies.

but now we walk
unhidden, revealing
the bleeding skin
to all who dare
to gaze upon us

and shudder.

look at our wounds!

see what we've lost
and lose each night.

life flows from gaping
flesh, staining clothes
and bed sheets.

we
leave
a
trail

everywhere we go.
follow us; understand

our agony.

each breath is alchemy

we are living alchemy.

we decay and transform within each instant.
from one phase to another, perpetually,

without end.

Dionysian Theatre

O Aeschylus

inform me of the mysteries
occulted within the text
of your tragedies.

is the secret not to enter the self;
to discover the self;
to see our suffering as an element

of transformation?

community

to lift each other
from dark waters

to relish in another's
triumph and happiness

to share stories of grief,
success, loneliness,
love.

to be accepted for who
you are, and for differences
to be celebrated.

this is what we all deserve.

Warmth

the opposite of negativity
is not positivity, but warmth.

when a person suffers,
provide:

an embrace. a walk.
a trip to the ice cream
store. crying together.
sitting in silence, simply
existing.

projection

the sky screams that I don't deserve to live.

Pierre is grateful I buy poutine from him
every day, but secretly wonders how
much longer until I have a heart attack.

each face I pass grimaces in disgust.

every mirror tells me I need to lose weight.

each phone call or message condemns
my irritating presence.

the cashier at the grocery store
asks me what day I plan to hang myself.

samsara

a perpetual cycle

where I perish and am reborn
in every passing moment

and, with each
death and each birth,

I catch another fleeting
glimpse of the True Being.

I am a part of it, like
all of you and all things.

and one day we shall
return to it, and we

will finally be free.

Revolution, or, the primordial art of Pyromancy

the Revolution is a hermaphrodite.

and when the Revolution comes,
a rain of fire shall burn away our
hatred, worries, and dreams.

this fire will annihilate everything.

all will be reduced to its pure, base
form: a perpetual force of matter
and energy that can never be
created or destroyed; only

transformed.

invocation

worship of the One
will shrivel this illusion
and reveal the true nature
of Everything.

treatment plan

Monday.
Wednesday.
Friday.

the procedure will occur
on these days, for four
weeks (approximately).

intermittent followup sessions
may be required, for maximum
efficacy.

there is always the possibility
that it will not be successful.

circle of protection

with salt I form a
circle around myself

to ward off demons
and all calamities.

an unexpected result
is that it repels even
the things I love.

my fear of harm has negated
the capacity to experience
anything, and

I slowly turn to bones.

sabotage

*"you try desperately,
but there is no escape
from us.*

*we control your thoughts;
your feelings; everything
you perceive.*

*and now we have proven
that we can manipulate
reality, itself.*

you will never receive ECT."

an ode to Jacques Prevel

was it your doom? that fateful moment
your path crossed with Antonin Artaud?

known only for your journal,
we are at last discovering
the poems you carved into
your very soul:

poems that speak in the sacred language of anguish.
anguish that is both universal and personal in nature.

anguish without which there would be nothing.

yet this anguish is not *everything*, and I hope to open
your eyes to the magic and beauty that is everywhere.

cruelty and transformation

I gazed upon their visage, ravaged and shaped by the march of time. And in the crevices of that face, I saw a lifetime of pain and joy, both radiant and blinding like the sun.

when the sky opens our fear will be gone

bend not in fear, but rejoice in our ascension:

liberated from bones and cities black as the void --
screaming colour back into the world as we break
off from decrepit skeletal stalks; jettisoned into a
nebulous sky to become celestial seeds searching
for each other in a vast sea of astral pollen.

and perhaps, one day, there will be
someone new to watch us shining.

the war against psychosis

the beings torment me from all sides.

they claim to control everything,
yet I have discovered a secret Flame
hidden within the layers of my illness.

and this Flame shall proceed from my mouth:

and in turn, it shall become my sword;
I shall wield it, with fury and with hope;

and I shall slay these beings once and for all.

all paths converge towards the Absolute

there are two things we all
secretly and unanimously
crave:

a sense of purpose, and
a sense of belonging.

by rediscovering the Absolute,
that we are all the Universe
experiencing itself,

we will love ourselves and each other
and no one will feel alone, anymore.

mortal coil

I, as you know me

(my form and mind,
 my passion and fear)

will cease to be.

 but all that I consist of,
my matter and my energy,

are eternal and return
to the cycles that form
existence.

and in this way, no
one ever truly dies.

Night Battles

each night,

in the darkest depths of myself,
I am battling diabolical witches.

their blood spills and my blood
spills and we revel in the carnage.

now that I have witnessed them bleed,
I am determined to see if they can die.

all I know is that soon the sun will rise.

poetry, or, a necessary immolation

I clad myself in a dark robe;
walk, with determination,
to the town square.

it is midnight.

I ring a brass bell
as I tread; not to
summon, but as
a warning, as if
to say,

"listen and be afraid.

watch, from the comfort
of your warm and cozy
home, the atrocity I am
about to commit."

in my right hand I carry
a container filled with fuel.

when I reach the centre
of town I cease the ringing
of my bell.

I stand, head bowed, in silence.

I reaffirm, in my mind, that
this is a necessary act.

I bathe myself in fuel
and, with the strike
of a match and a single,
resounding scream,

I light up their world.

In the presence of the Absolute

I am floating through the air.
I turn and embrace the sublime.

all my being dissolves, returns
to the force that is everything.

a hazy, waking dream.
I bask in the most beautiful
thing I have ever seen.

acknowledgments:

cover art by Graham Cwinn
author photo by Shannon Duncan (Level Up Photography)

special thanks: Max, Liam, Sara H, Evan, Brendan, Savannah, Reed, Julien, Rosie, John, Dave, Shawn, Kyle, Sara Y, Shannon, Maeve, Blake, my family, and everyone else who has supported me on my darkest and brightest days.

Published by Things in my Chest
Copyright © Graham Cwinn 2023

ISBN: 978-1-7389800-2-4

thingsinmychest.com

about the author

Graham Cwinn is an author, artist, and musician living in Ottawa, Ontario. He has self-published several poetry collections, a short story, and is writing and illustrating a graphic novel. Graham also runs the small press Things in my Chest. His work offers glimmers of hope in the face of schizoaffective disorder, trauma, and loss.

other works by Graham Cwinn

Tangled Thoughts of Leaving

hiraeth - listen carefully to hearts breaking.

Crawl Inside

"one day all this will end."

the flesh is not a prison

my neighbour wants to kill me

the shape of my will

www.ingramcontent.com/pod-product-compliance
Lightning Source LLC
Chambersburg PA
CBHW071509080526
44587CB00016B/2732